Dogs

# Bulldogs

## by Jody Sullivan Rake
Consulting Editor: Gail Saunders-Smith, PhD

Consultant: Jennifer Zablotny, DVM
Member, American Veterinary Medical Association

Capstone
press
Mankato, Minnesota

Pebble Books are published by Capstone Press,
151 Good Counsel Drive, P.O. Box 669, Mankato, Minnesota 56002.
www.capstonepress.com

1 2 3 4 5 6 12 11 10 09 08 07

*Library of Congress Cataloging-in-Publication Data*
Rake, Jody Sullivan.
    Bulldogs / by Jody Sullivan Rake.
    p. cm.—(Pebble Books. Dogs)
    Summary: "Simple text and photographs present an introduction to the bulldog
breed, its growth from puppy to adult, and pet care information"—Provided
by publisher.
    Includes bibliographical references and index.
    ISBN-13: 978-1-4296-0014-9 (hardcover)
    ISBN-10: 1-4296-0014-4 (hardcover)
    1. Bulldog—Juvenile literature. I. Title. II. Series.
SF429.B85R35 2008
636.72—dc22                                      2006100730

## Note to Parents and Teachers

The Dogs set supports national science standards related to life
science. This book describes and illustrates bulldogs. The images
support early readers in understanding the text. The repetition of
words and phrases helps early readers learn new words. This book
also introduces early readers to subject-specific vocabulary words,
which are defined in the Glossary section. Early readers may need
assistance to read some words and to use the Table of Contents,
Glossary, Read More, Internet Sites, and Index sections of the book.

# Table of Contents

# Tough and Tender

Bulldogs' faces
make them look tough.
But they are gentle
and loving pets.

Bulldogs make
good watchdogs.
They bravely protect
their owners
from strangers.

# From Puppy to Adult

Bulldogs have four or five puppies in a litter.
The tiny puppies
have large heads.

Bulldog puppies like
to chew on toys.
Bulldogs still like chewing
when they are adults.

Adult bulldogs are short and heavy. Bulldogs are half as tall as a coffee table.

# Taking Care of Bulldogs

Bulldogs need food
and water every day.
Bulldogs need
two short walks
every day.

Bulldogs' wrinkly faces
get dirty easily.
Clean your bulldog's face
with a cotton ball
or a cloth everyday.

Bulldogs have trouble
breathing on hot days.
Keep them inside
near a fan to stay cool.

Bulldogs may look mean. But they are gentle dogs that need lots of love.

# Glossary

brave—showing courage and willingness to do difficult things

gentle—kind and calm

litter—a group of animals born at one time to the same mother

protect—to keep safe from danger

tough—dangerous or mean

watchdog—a dog trained to guard a house, property or people

wrinkles—covered with lines or folds

# Read More

Fiedler, Julie. *Bulldogs.* Tough Dogs. New York: PowerKids Press, 2006.

Frisch, Joy. *Bulldogs.* Dog Breeds. North Mankato, Minn.: Smart Apple Media, 2003.

# Internet Sites

FactHound offers a safe, fun way to find Internet sites related to this book. All of the sites on FactHound have been researched by our staff.

Here's how:

1. Visit *www.facthound.com*

2. Choose your grade level.

3. Type in this book ID **1429600144** for age-appropriate sites. You may also browse subjects by clicking on letters, or by clicking on pictures and words.

4. Click on the **Fetch It** button.

**FactHound will fetch the best sites for you!**

# Index

Word Count: 133
Grade: 1
Early-Intervention Level: 18

**Editorial Credits**

Becky Viaene, editor; Juliette Peters, set designer; Kim Brown, book designer;
Kara Birr, photo researcher; Karon Dubke, photographer; Kelly Garvin, photo stylist

**Photo Credits**

Capstone Press/Karon Dubke, 12, 14, 16, 18, 20; Istock Photo/farbenrausch, 6;
Mark Raycroft, cover; Norvia Behling/Daniel Johnson, 10; Shutterstock/Claudia
Steininger, 1; Shutterstock/Michael Scott Bessler, 4; SuperStock, Inc., 8

Capstone Press thanks dog trainer Martha Diedrich for her assistance with this book.